The Speed Flyers

by
Jonny Zucker

illustrated by
David Shephard

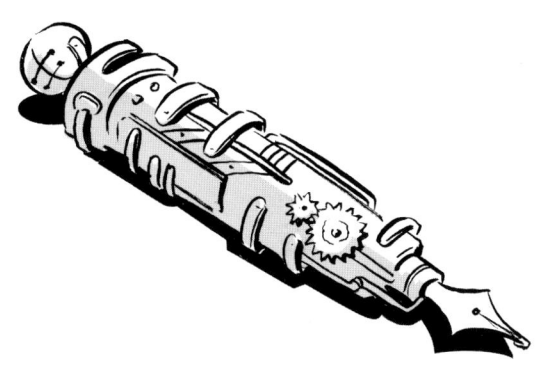

First Flight

Titles in More First Flight

Comic Chaos	Jonny Zucker
Into The Deep	Jonny Zucker
Cyber Phone	Richard Taylor
Mutt	Jane A C West
Captured!	Alison Hawes
Robot Goalie	Roger Hurn
Alien Eggs	Danny Pearson
Just in Time	Jane A C West
The Speed Flyers	Jonny Zucker
Super Teacher	Stan Cullimore

Badger Publishing Limited
Suite G08, Business & Technology Centre
Bessemer Drive, Stevenage, Hertfordshire SG1 2DX
Telephone: 01438 791037   Fax: 01438 791036
www.badger-publishing.co.uk

The Speed Flyers ISBN 978-1-84926-458-7

Text © Jonny Zucker 2011
Complete work © Badger Publishing Limited 2011

All rights reserved. No part of this publication may be reproduced, stored in any form or by any means mechanical, electronic, recording or otherwise without the prior permission of the publisher.

The right of Jonny Zucker to be identified as author of this Work has been asserted by him in accordance with the Copyright, Designs and Patents Act 1988.

Badger Publishing would like to thank Jonny Zucker for his help in putting this series together.

Publisher: David Jamieson
Senior Editor: Danny Pearson
Design: Fiona Grant
Illustration: David Shephard

The Speed Flyers

Contents

Chapter 1	History	page 5
Chapter 2	The Palace	page 9
Chapter 3	Anne Boleyn	page 13
Chapter 4	Mrs Crust	page 17
Chapter 5	Over Here!	page 23
Henry VIII		page 30
Questions		page 32

New words:

twinkling commanded
museum palace
hesitated throne

Main characters:

Mr Blast

Stacey

Kevin

Chapter 1
History

Mr Blast was Kevin and Stacey's new History teacher.

He had a long beard and twinkling blue eyes.

At the start of his first lesson, he carried a large, purple carpet into the classroom.

"Today we will be learning about King Henry VIII," he said.

Kevin, Stacey and the rest of the class got out their History text books, but Mr Blast shook his head. "You will not need any text books today," he told them. "I believe you should learn History first hand. So you will just need a sketch pad and a pen."

"Are we going to a museum?" asked Stacey.

"We are going somewhere far more exciting than a museum," grinned Mr Blast. "Can you please come and sit on the carpet?"

Everyone left their tables and sat on the carpet. It was thick and very comfortable.

Mr Blast threw a window open.

"What are you doing?" asked Stacey.

But Mr Blast did not answer. Instead, he came to sit on the carpet. "Everyone ready?" he called.

"For what?" cried the class.

Mr Blast tapped his pen three times on the carpet. For a few seconds nothing happened. But then the carpet rose into the air.

Everyone in the class screamed, including Kevin and Stacey.

At that second, the head teacher, Mrs Crust came into the room. She looked in shock at the hovering carpet.

"COME DOWN NOW!" she commanded.

But she was too late. The carpet made a hissing noise and zoomed out of the window.

Chapter 2
The Palace

"Do not worry!" shouted Mr Blast, at the screaming children. "There is an invisible force field around the carpet that stops you falling off."

Kevin reached out his hand and touched a solid wall at the carpet's edge.

"Hold on tight!" cried Mr Blast.

The carpet flew up into the clouds at amazing speed. For a few seconds, no one could see anything, but then the carpet swooped down.

It landed in a large field next to a large and very grand palace.

Everyone got off the carpet.

Up ahead, some people in old-fashioned clothes were walking into the palace.

"Welcome to the 16th century!" beamed Mr Blast.

"You are joking!" cried Stacey.

But Mr Blast shook his head. "I will show you around first," he said. "And then there's someone I'd like you to meet."

Mr Blast took the class on a tour of the palace. They saw the tennis-court, the well, the amazing gardens and the weapons store. Everyone made notes and drew sketches.

"This is amazing!" gasped Kevin, gazing at a huge silver sword.

"We will now go inside the palace," said Mr Blast.

They walked into a huge corridor that had large paintings of angels and musicians on the walls. The corridor led to the throne room.

At the far end someone was sitting on the throne. . .

It was King Henry VIII.

Chapter 3
Anne Boleyn

"Greetings to you!" roared the King. "You are the group who are touring here before going to the be-heading at the Tower later today?"

"Yes we are," answered Mr Blast, bowing to the King.

Stacey, Kevin and the others bowed too.

"Your clothes are strange," said the King. "And that reminds me. Would someone help me on with this jacket?"

"We will!" said Stacey, grabbing Kevin by the elbow.

They ran over and started helping him.

When the jacket was on, Kevin held his sketch pad and pen up. "Would you mind signing this?" he asked.

Henry took the pen in his hand. "What kind of writing tool is this?" he asked.

"It's a pen," replied Kevin.

"I like it!" boomed the King, signing his name.

"I need to look at some papers," declared Henry. "I will see you all later at the be-heading!"

He swept out of the room.

Mr Blast led the class out of the throne room and back down the corridor. They were about to go outside when they heard a knocking sound from behind the wall.

Kevin touched the wall and a secret door suddenly slid open.

A very pale woman appeared.

She looked very frightened.

"I am Anne Boleyn," she whispered, looking in terror down the corridor. "If you do not help me, I will be dead by the end of the day!"

At that moment there was a loud shout from the throne room.

At the end of the corridor they saw Henry VIII with a gang of soldiers. "THERE SHE IS!" yelled the King.

Mr Blast looked at them for a second and then shouted, "RUN!"

Chapter 4
Mrs Crust

"STOP!" screamed King Henry as he and his soldiers raced down the corridor.

But Mr Blast, Anne Boleyn and the class did not stop. They ran outside and kept running until they had reached the carpet. They all jumped on it.

The King and his soldiers got nearer and nearer.

Mr Blast tapped his pen three times on the carpet but nothing happened.

"COME ON!" yelled Anne.

Mr Blast saw that his pen was upside down. He flipped it round, and tapped it three times.

The carpet flew upwards.

Henry managed to grab the edge of the carpet. "COME BACK HERE!" he screamed.

But Kevin gave his hand a good kick. The King yelled and let go.

The carpet flew up into the clouds.

For a few seconds, no one could see anything, but when they came out of the clouds, they saw their school below them.

The carpet flew in through the open window.

Mrs Crust was waiting for them.
She looked very, very angry.
"WHERE ON EARTH HAVE YOU BEEN?" she cried.

"We've been back to the 16th century," replied Stacey.

"We met King Henry VIII!" said Kevin, holding up the King's autograph.

"And I suppose she is Anne Boleyn?" sneered Mrs Crust looking at the woman in old-fashioned clothes, sitting next to Mr Blast on the carpet.

"Nice to meet you," said Anne, stepping off the carpet.

"This is just a trick!" said Mrs Crust. "No one can go back in time and meet Henry VIII."

"Come with us and I will show you," said Mr Blast.

Mrs Crust hesitated. "OK," she finally said. "Is she coming with us?"
She pointed at Anne.

"No," replied Mr Crust, "If she comes back she may lose her head."

Mrs Crust sat down on the carpet. "I still don't believe you," she said, coldly.

Mr Blast tapped his pen three times and the carpet shot out of the window.

Mrs Crust screamed in terror.

Five minutes later, the carpet was flying down into the field beside the palace.

Mrs Crust tried to speak but she was so shocked that no words came out.

Chapter 5
Over Here!

Mr Blast and his pupils showed Mrs Crust all round the palace. She stared at everything with amazement.

They were walking in the palace gardens when they heard a shout. "There they are!"

It was Henry VIII and his soldiers.

As the King and his soldiers marched towards them, Stacey and Kevin snuck away. Mr Blast, Mrs Crust and the pupils suddenly found themselves in a dead end.

"WHERE IS ANNE BOLEYN?" yelled Henry.

"She's gone from your horrible clutches!" replied Mrs Crust.

"WHO ARE YOU?" demanded Henry, staring at Mrs Crust in wonder.

"I am Elizabeth Crust!" she replied.

"If Anne has gone, you will be my new Queen!" declared Henry VIII. "We shall marry in the morning!"

The soldiers moved to grab her but at that second, Kevin and Stacey appeared.

"OVER HERE!" they shouted.

The King and his soldiers spun round.

As soon as they did this, Kevin and Stacey started whacking tennis balls at them with the rackets they'd borrowed from the tennis court.

All of the soldiers and King Henry were knocked onto the ground.

"MOVE!" shouted Mr Blast, jumping over the King and his soldiers. Everyone followed him.

"THIS WAY!" shouted Kevin and Stacey, racing back to the carpet.

Henry and his soldiers were now on their feet and chasing them.

Everyone jumped onto the carpet.

Mr Blast tapped his pen three times and the carpet rose into the air.

Henry VIII caught up with them and grabbed the carpet. But Stacey bit his hand and he let go with a howl.

The carpet flew into the clouds.

Five minutes later they were back in school.

"That was amazing!" said Mrs Crust. "I'm so sorry I did not believe you."

"No problem!" smiled Mr Blast.

Mrs Crust turned to face Anne Boleyn who was sitting on Mr Blast's desk. "What would you like to do now?" Mrs Crust asked Anne kindly.

"I would like to stay here," replied Anne, "but I don't know what I could do."

Kevin ran to Mrs Crust and whispered something in her ear.

A school newsletter was sent home that night.

One item caught Kevin and Stacey's eye. It announced that the school had a new dinner lady.

Her name? Miss Boleyn.

Henry VIII

*King Henry VIII had two of his wives be-headed. Anne Boleyn was the first, Kathryn Howard was second.
The be-headings took place at the Tower of London.*

Henry lived at Hampton Court Palace. Lots of the things that were there when he was alive, are still there; like the tennis court and the ornate gardens.

Many films and TV shows have been made about Henry VIII.

William Shakespeare wrote a play called Henry VIII. This was first performed in 1613.

Henry the VIII was born on the 28th June 1491.
He died on the 28th January 1547.

Questions

- *In what way is the carpet safe?*

- *What is Henry VIII planning for the day?*

- *Why is Anne Boleyn so keen for Mr Blast and his pupils to help her?*

- *What does Kevin show Mrs Crust to make her believe the class really have been back to the 16th century?*

- *What does Henry want to do with Mrs Crust?*